Air into Breath

Poems by

Kathryn Winograd

The Ashland Poetry Press
Ashland University
Ashland, Ohio 44805

Acknowledgment is made to the following journals and anthologies for poems that have appeared previously in their pages:

The Antioch Review : "Winter Betrothal"
Anthology of Magazine Verse & Yearbook of American Poetry: "It Is Spring, Yes"
Appalachian: *"Snow drifts in the shadow..."* (published under the title, "Spring River")
Chester H. Jones Award: "What's Already Lost"
Cincinnati Poetry Review : "In a Country We Didn't Know"
Colorado Review : "Receiving the Father's Love"
The Denver Quarterly : "Sleeping with Our Daughters," "Dark Birds" (published under the title, "Night Prayer")
Farmer's Market: "It Is Spring, Yes," "To Where There's Never Been"
The Journal: "Mira's Dream"
Kalliope: "At the Ruins of the Aztec Goddess Ix-Chel," "Day of Atonement"
Many Mountains Moving: "The Weasel Sandman"
New Virginia Review: "Light Gazers"
The New Yorker: "Before Nightfall"
The Ohio Review: "Infecundity"
Perceptions: "Early Labors"
Poets Lore: "How the Moon Saves Us from Chaotic Tilting"
Poets On: "Roto-Rooter Man"
Sow's Ear Poetry Review: "How Stories Would Change Us," "River Swim"
TriQuarterly: "Finch Nested"
Weber Studies: "Blizzard," "Family Alzheimer's," Early Labors"
Water Stone: "Incubations"
Xanadu: "Easter Amid the Orthodox"

Thanks also to the Colorado Council on the Arts for a grant that supported the writing of portions of this book.

Printed in the United States of America

ISBN: 0-912592-48-6

Library of Congress Catalog Card Number: 2002101233

Cover art: Trine Bumiller, "Plover"
Cover design: Micki Amick

In memory and love
to my father--

In love
to those who live with me still

Contents

I

I understand there is no river here
winter or other

nor the red dirt
of my daughter's skin
beautiful to my touch

in the rain-hail
nor a thousand yellow flowers

breaking

But we are like those bodies
far north frozen above tundra

no one can bury

Think of what we have not said—
your snow and our secrets
beneath the skin

of snow

The wind winds its long body
around us

and the nimbus moon
curves
beneath a bruise

Finch Nested

I

Finch nested, I could not help myself
pulling down again and again
      that half globe of earth
studded by petunia, purpling flag
of the heart's bowl.

I disturbed air. I lessened heat
sometimes my rooting there
      pitched like a wound
in the eye's seed
in that dark helmet of finch head,

bird I waved into the green
unfolding. What does it mean then
      to have taken into my hands
this potted plant with its nested finch
as if it were you

or yours or this whole
long winter, your flowers of winter?
      And to hold on to it
as if you were standing at some river now
forgetting everything

and me, saying over and over again
before the mind sits only the world?

II

Everything we do is alone,
in loneliness, such
      quiet.
Here, I say to my daughters
again and again, *three blue finch eggs*
and now it is not you,
but your mother I hold.
     Already my hands,
their long bones you have given me,
bend as hers did in her leaving,

their whiteness
like the first stars in the hard
     light we cling to.
Thumb size, blue tombs of the sky,
our falterings—paradisical—freckle,

here are the shells
the singing bone leaches
     in dark genetic storm, small bird pulse.
And now we watch the crossing over—
sac of the body, the vein's web, bird blossoming.

III

Resurrection. My father.
I wanted only to save them, what
     my quiet watching
had already damned, finch fled now,
and I, like some Christ with a Q tip,

filling its nestlings with sugar water.
They opened their mouths to me,
        all beak and dark throat,
soundless what spurs the mother.
And then the black bulge of their hearts

stopped.
How the world blurs—
        my mother weeping, wood
of my ailing father
burgeoning, all those black clusters

of trees, how can I name them?
Like shrouds their branches   .
        in the winterlight
spill down and the snow crusted and finch,
I mean, cardinal (the betraying

brain, oh, wounding) burn
where my father—
        Bird-Blossomer,
River-Swallowing-Snow—
already walks.

Family Alzheimer's

If we could still speak only of stars, of blue
lights, the earth's unsteadying. Or of the deer
you love—the nights rural—their blind
leaping past the fences into your white light.

How must you see your own body,
physician, you who have stitched even my
white bones, pulled even me
from woman clay, dust, leaf of the garden
        into the wide moon's ebb?

I must speak of anything else now:
not bone nor moon nor of your body, its
darkness, my fragile shell, my father, your
heart grasped and the great emptiness
        of air moving in and through.

This is how the brain leaves us:
out of the genetic earth, out of the ploughed
field, glacial furrow, rock volcanic.
There is a half-tunnel our mothers, our fathers
have dug for us. Dirt clings to them. Their spines
        curl embryonic.

This is no dream. The moon sways. You
cannot feel the air, say "air" but the blinds
trill, moon-light chattering down the gut.
My father, you fumble at the gate.
        It is your mother I am thinking of,

chin to the knee, thumb to the palm curling, all
the world a speechless dusk.
I understand it like this: the body mute
nets the bright tissue of the brain,
          moon in slices.

The brain wants to return to its beginnings:
budding stem, amphibian, cleft of gill.
You whirl. You click softly. This
is what we understand, but do you know
already what I cannot say?
          what I cannot speak?

My father, I am standing with you
at the mouth of the earth. I am feeling
the small rains, the dazed stars pitched and dimming, you
who I love, my tongue
          already cut.

How Stories Would Change Us

I could tell it so simply,
children in a creek playing, sunlight
breaking over them, those glints of gold.
Or how for once it seemed he was almost
happy, the boy we always hated as children hate—
blind and animal—this day playing beside us,
the slippery fish of his hands
darting through those brief shots of sunlight
a wood allows, turning stone after stone,
whole forests, I think, whole worlds,
those lost veins, those fixed blue houses
of bone felled again and again in the turning.

I remember the water shuddered like beaten tin,
that creek the storm-wash of our own streets
ebbing down through gutters, down through those lightless
sewers, the darkness we half-entered.
This story should end here.
But what do you do with a day's end when a father
strips his eldest son and sends him
diapered and beaten into the fetid dusk
of summer for show? And what do you do when the boy
you always hated stands weeping in the last gasps
of heat rising from those dark skids of blacktop
and you cannot breathe and the whole world
wavers in front of you, bent and fix-less?

Understand there's no ending in this.
Think dusk and one by one the lighted trees
of any summer are riven into sheathes of dusk.
The shimmering street tar of any day
sinks into lightlessness, dusk no burial

but a resurrection, oared and vagrant,
its long low skiffs skimming over the sudden wakes
of grass, the glass-glitter of forgotten streets,
those dream-shards we call our children
returning stained and weary to us
as we lay our bodies down in the same dark,
to dream the same dream, the same house,
the same mother lying white and suicidal in the dark,
begging for death as she always does.
And her son, whom we never once thought not to hate,
bends to fail her again and again, to kiss the heart
once more into its relentless filling.

Light Gazers

How many winters through the thinned trees
would I watch from my window
$\qquad$ the blue-hill drift of light,
the one room schoolhouse where my father would go
to heal no one but to lay his hands without hope
$\qquad$ over the slow waste of a man
made crippled by some errant desire, his great wreck—
that scoured patch of field and the car that thrust his body
from him—

$\qquad\qquad\qquad$ grown long over?

It was nothing I saw but what my father told me,
riding in evening loose-kneed the taut back
$\qquad$ of my sister's snap-eyed, barn-soured
horse,
red smoke of our dirt road hanging
where he'd come straight from the last burn of the sun,
$\qquad\qquad$ round and eye-able
as an August-swell of moon.
I would imagine myself in it:
$\qquad$ the man, the wheelchair that was his
body,

the fat sad wife he cursed, his gray children
and the brother we called Jesus
$\qquad\qquad$ who loved him,
who night after night thundered the dark air
as he sped past the invisible fields,
$\qquad$ and dreamed this crippled man whole again—
his body in summer floating
like pale flowers at midnight as the last houselights
$\qquad\qquad$ skitter black-winged

over a smooth expanse of pond—
this dream breaking always beneath the weight
                    of this man who falls drunk from his chair
to float weeping in water
over the stilled weight of his legs,
                    and can ask for nothing more
than the warmth and the water rushing into him
and those mapped stars traveling once more above him
                    elusive, past air.

There is a woman who lives in the streets of my block
sleeping now, the light of my porch
                    sifting weakly like breath in winter
over her arms and her face bent into shadow.
All day she has driven her life freely over the city,
                    the seeable spaces of her car
filled with the trash and the tattered castoffs
she has laid down into dumpsters for and built into this:
          some life overwhelming.

I could go out to her.
I could open this door and let the house throw out
                    its long wedge of light
and walk then in quiet to the street's edge
and with the same desire
of the man who once stole through the silent summer
grass to stroke a woman in dream—
her legs fallen and senseless in the sunlight—
touch the cold glass where she breathes.

Receiving the Father's Love
to A.D.

I cannot walk with you in air
nor see how the heather, the rough stalks of sea
in your desert chill whitens, ossifies.

Within you there is a wounding.
The dream that is your father hangs
above you night after night in rafters, bundled, mute.

What I know is what I know of my own:
the smooth water of his skin over those thin bones
that want the turn of stone.

How can our fathers love us as we want?
For so long we have ridden the ship of our mothers.
We are the blue veins that rivered their breasts,

our mothers lying on their backs in narrow beds,
their bellies rising full-mooned,
while the nurse attending waves her magic wand

to plumb the depths of a ticking sea, our hearts
the tiny beacon-flash that our mothers,
our blood and breath, searched for.

And, there, in the small screen of the sonogram,
echoing the soft no bones of our bodies,
our reflected fathers, peripheral, hovering.

Yes, our fathers are the dream.
They wade through the long bones of ponies—
those clean tunneling stars—our fathers

the single lights that sail beneath the night loam,
break over the blue lights of our new fields,
wild and long-stemmed.

And now you have come to see me.
We sit on quiet red hillsides, grasses
crumpling beneath our backs, the day moon's shell,

its cusp, floating above us.
We cannot say how we are lonely.
I want to ask you: Do you the woman

because you cannot love the father?
You see, Annie, when I finally did,
it was at my father's feet, my daughter fallen

bleeding, and I held her weeping in my arms
and then gave her wholly to my father.
It is a sweet death.

Only he could save her, only he could blow back
into her lungs *Come into this world* his breath,
our breath *Here are the bones* his love

and they are air and lace
what I had always wanted. Our fathers thin.
They are the dreams that dream.

Soon they will hardly know us.
What is the heart?
Flapping valve, branched muscle,

the soul's seat beneath the white armor
of the taken rib, pulse,
its weavings, the spider tremors beneath our skins.

Already the stone ax sleeps beneath a rain of hyacinth
and now it is my daughter who breathes
and I lay my head upon her heart.

It is he who knocks.

How the Moon Saves Us from Chaotic Tilting

You are large and round. The full moon
of your belly eclipses the loosened
buckle of your belt. You are painting
your brown house green. It is winter's brown,
the walnut's hull split and staining,
and you are painting it green, not spring's
verdant, the sunning lizard's changed
back, but fall's, summer's smoke.
Your wife helps you. We wave to one another.

It is perfect here, the garden's mirror.
We have pinned our fences to the air, sown blue
the wire grasses, spilled our bags of loam
and sheep dung, the sun-hewn bark
over the seepless clay,
over the still bone-float of horses
and ancient sea camels,
the butcher's chipped flints.
We have housed in our cottonwoods
cleaned sunflower, thistle, cracked barley.
Our yards fill with sparrow, thrush, grackle.
Over our heads blue heron, magpie, the raptor
drift pushed and floating.
Our gardens flicker.

We prune, we shear, we transplant.
We wave to one another. I wave to you.
You are painting your brown house almost green
and your wife helps you. And now the arced moon
billows over the fences of the schoolyard.
Broke, our children tell us. *The moon broke.*
We sleep in our beds spent without touching.

Outside our windows, the heated flickers
drill the gutterspouts.

The brown house almost green,
you stand in your kitchen now, order carefully
on your kitchen counter the wallet that names you, the
keys that lock and unlock you, your notes to family.
You collect from your swept garage
your neat loops of hoses.
I wave to you. You wave to me.
You drive carefully past muffled plains, small wild rivers.
You enter old parking lots.
You fasten your hose to your muffler.
We hear the wind chink, the wild peacock.

I watched you painting
your brown house green and now your wife
lets down the white door
of her station wagon, and the gold buttons
of the chrysanthemum
slide into the world.

Easter Amid the Orthodox

If I could think only *yes*.
Spring, and as always, without You,
I bend my weight into the earth, as if forgiven
of this garden, to shovel it dark and good
into the floating light
where all winter the stiff ribs of my lilacs
lay down quiet in blue snow.
Blade after blade, the slumbered soil
drifts through the air and covers me lightly.
Beneath me, the first shades of birds,
beckoned and lonely,
shed their wings over the real, the unimagined,
this press of peat and bone
where the wintered staff of the onion
skews crookedly toward sky, and broken
bits of china, where once
the happy faces of women floated pale and full
in the slow ebb of their own breath,
rain down their shattered roses.
My neighbor has come out
into the last slants of light to work her garden.
I think I can never forget how lightly,
with so much joy
she runs her hands over the fresh paint
of her walls she calls satin,
or how, more than seasonal, she balances
on the shaky rungs of some ladder to polish endlessly
winter or summer or the imagined nothings
of any moment from her window.
Soon she will come to greet me,
 and we will speak as neighbors speak
across a fence, amid lilac,

the still lives of ourselves suspended
for a moment in that last sun, the sky
that wash of peach amid the gleaming.
Hers is an old garden,
and she thinks to harvest into air all it holds.
A simple lifting of her sleeve, and magic,
the flat of her arm, tattooed,
holds the tripled moon like blue shadow
across the snow, and old,
the woman bends to scrape her perfect lawn
into furrows imagined, her hoe imagined,
and beckoned, that dead garden
spills dark and sour over the spring roots,
potatoes like stumps.
As close as you, she'll say, this gardener of Auschwitz,
I could see everything,
and, darkness like a dome,
she unseals for me the remembered fire
and the body, Love,
soon to shut us out, shrinks and burn.

Owl-Light

It is a failing of direction, this.
To think I could ever again

walk out of these woods and say
this mine, this earth, this now.

Already the owl sings
at the long house of my father.

This is not the river, but its bend,
old woods ice-snapped, Milky Way

of our fathers' fathers teetering
over me as if it were still the end

to everything: space, world, being—
that long, tethering light.

I have come to look for owl, that winged
shadow of my childhood, silence

rushing through me.
I scan the trees for their roostings, their winter

couplings. I hear the wires overhead
hiss with the snow's weight.

Iron burrs stagger in the wind.
Delicate bones scatter at my feet.

(Is this my only happiness?)

Here is even winter's death, snow
as if the air broke and a moon of ice

rode over my light skin.
Sometimes they will come wheeling

out of the sky, a brilliant slashing
of air and knock you to the ground,

blind, strike talon-deep for anyone's heart.
And then the blood stirs.

The very hollows of the bones heat
and the owls fly into one another.

Here is the spring
before the very coldest of springs—

my father dead and everything,
everyone I ever thought loved

(even you) unchanged.
Bring me the heart of the owl

and let it sleep upon my sleeping
woman's heart. It is all dark

prophet, horn and stone.
It will tell you everything.

Field Questionnaire for the Fossil Hunter
from The Fossil Book

1. *Are there any noteworthy growth forms;*
such as delicately branched coral?

Our fathers are old or think they are old.
The earth tips like a wave.
It does not turn in the wind-tide.
The long crooked bones
of strangers hang from our rafters.

2. *Are there any possible peculiarities of adaptation?*

We have come to see the tracks
of dinosaurs. I have given him
my daughters to carry.
They stand at the fence
hand in hand. Our daughters' eyes
tilt like strange oceans
our fathers will not travel.

3. *Are there any obviously pathological specimens*
or any that have been damaged during life?

They are spines and dark plums.
Out of the blown earth,
these tracks climb and climb.
We want to say to our fathers
that it is as easy as stepping
into water.
How the hollow rushes spiral down

weighty, collective.
And then the sea,
its ancient salts.

*4. Are there any signs of seasonal growth or of
general change in growth or direction during life?*

In long yellow fields, our fathers
wade through the sea-drift, the blue
casts of mollusk and snail, the wishbone
and its pores.

5. Are there any fossils in positions of life?

I am his daughter
and I stand at my daughter's bed.
It is dark. Her bones are small
and light. Outside the snow, volcanic,
imprints the last leafs
and the lifeless moon
fills the whole house
with its light,
and everyone sleeps.

II

Here is not spring's ease,
soft mouth flower,
Golden Eye of August.

Everything has bent
and gone under,

the river green
I cannot find it
in some far tundra locked.

(You are all I think of now, all).

I carry the flowers
of winter-stick leaf
and musk thistle, houndstongue.

Where are the birds
in light step
beneath the star's spin?

Where the bee
in numbed sleep
beneath the wax?

Here is a pod
closed as the heart.

Inside it is all damp
spider skein
and cusp of seed—

dark thumbnails
the air cannot hold.

What's Already Lost

On water greener
          than the wavering banks we whirlpool down
          through the lake's still surface,
we circle around and around on the pink shell of the house,
our boat gliding in and out of the windows,
over the many faces of my family
          that wink and twirl like lures
                    cast in and out of the depths.

We are here for a wedding,
          a final leaving of what's already lost,
                    this girl I was and I
combing the lockless oars through the long spaces
between us, the white flower of her face
          in the wake beside me,
          in that other world
                    I cannot breathe in.

Except where her face
          sometimes opens everything,
          I cannot see down to the dark shapes
          I know swim past, momentary, then disappear,
the silty bottom breathing up in a sudden cloud,
and the moss that fingers by
          wrapping itself around the oars
          that will pass it into air and make it dust.

But this is hardly tragic. What of the women
before me, before any of us,
          virginal, dangled chastely over the teeming world,
          the final unveiling only then bringing to light
          what was always submerge?

The people I love are beginning to gather now.
Soon they will come to lift me,
      shining and netted from the lake.

Before Nightfall

Rain, and before nightfall,
the first creek waters will wash past this fence
and into the lower pasture, pooling
where cattle and horse once sunk to their hocks
in other storm, another year, our whole family
and the neighbor's up at the bellowing. I began then,
saving first a tooth cracked from some heifer's jaw
when I saw how our flashlights and pale, rain-caped faces
panicked them all, some falling to their knees,
some surging past to vanish uncaught, their heads
and hips lunging stiff-jointed from side to side.

I come here often to root under
the scattered rocks and long braids of pressed grass.
Mornings, I've sat in the middle of this ten-yard creek
on a rock dried by heat and tongue, the only water
taken by scum and spider, and found over the years
pieces of drowned crawfish, gutted, bubble-eyed,
the rock-dragged hulls of shredded creek mussel, black wings
of dragonflies spit back from the mouths of fish,
washed animal bones, even a snail's bloody-toothed shell,
petrified, thumb-worn, dropped from some pocket miles
          upstream.

I have kept them all in a brown jewelry box
I once found in our barn's farthest corner, its key
and lock rusted, unable to turn them safe. Early evening,
and I'm still out here hunting, my boots,
slapping down on the smooth-sheeted clay and pressed silt,
waffle-treaded, huge
among all the other tracks of other travelers,
theirs five-toed, long-heeled, broken-mooned,
the body above them barely weighted.

To Where There's Never Been

Today, in the barnyard's churned, hoof-pocked muck,
I found again those little new-moon slivers,
what we trim from the horse's hoof, once swept from us
and half-buried now beneath the tipped trough
and the stall's heavy swung door. I picked one up.
Thick where it bulged, and dark,
pearling to a center thin some places stained:
I knew it was from my horse's foundered foot,
that rim of rotted shell we'd sometimes slice too deep
and gash the oozy under.

The horse gone, I cupped his pieced foot in my hand
as if I could still clean the crumbling stark rind
beneath its wet coat of mud and straw,
pick pebble and loose thorn out from under its black
and lifting frog, the tender furred skin above the hoof
scarred and ridged by some pony's kick or creek's stumble-
stone that jagged it as he sucked, the worse lipped from
some tangle of hunter-sprung barb.

No one else yet, I'd lay my face to his,
look in and out of that clear, jelled bubble,
its gaped pupil already rooting, pulling him down,
and see fence and tree, sometimes my own face,
finally the whole family, swallowed, drowning
as they climbed gloved and bucketed past the gate
to where there's never been an old shoe left for luck
or tapped nail filed bright, and glittering the muddied ground.

Winter Betrothal

We have found a strange footprint
on the shores of the unknown.
                    —Sir Arthur Eddington

In New York, we once stood over Leakey's
"strange footprints from the shores of the unknown."
Smaller than ours, but ours, cast from the volcanic ash
they were frozen in, they walked side by side off the
plaster mold into a world we couldn't see, and turned once
to look back. I bring you here now to my once-home in Ohio
where my parents wave us to the fences, to yesterday's
skim of snow that marks the night's travelers,
the grounded bird's spiny toes that twig our path.
                    Winter, each separate limb of the woods

black against a low sun, the stretched legs of a spider
draw over us. In the frozen pond pocked by the burnt-down
stubble of cattails, stalks drying in heaps on the lit banks,
my father's decoys topple on a wave lifted now by no wind.
All around us is the clutter of what's been:
the stacked weathered boards of a bee box,
the row boat where rain once drowned a tumbled red-wing,
and hooked fish mouthed themselves dry at my feet on a
sunny day.
                    Somehow, I thought this would all be different,

that it would matter I was here with you, that I could say
yes, this is what I loved, but now...
then vanish, forget these tiny, punched-out tracks in the
snow that turn me and turn me. I remember the night we
drove to the fields in Texas to blink into sight the
returning of a comet barely there among all the stars we
could see fixed into that slow, down-flooding dark.

31

I could smell the rain as far away as here
rising out of the ground. Past the fences,
the horses rented to the fields will come down to greet us
and leave tracks that unbury the cold earth
                                and slip long tails into the snow.

In a Country We Didn't Know

I can't say it was love or marriage
that sent us stumbling down the rattling,
                root-forked banks of a creekbed,
in a country we didn't know or want to know,
only that we were alone,
                and the green scraped velvet from the
drowned rocks,
and the water cast summer skies that played and glinted
along the storm-scoured shelves we lay on.

Nothing romantic, nothing we'd call passion,
but duty, what's expected,
                like the first night of marriage:
everyone knowing, everyone dreaming of the coupled path,
the filled channel
                that will wash each one into eternity.

It was my scarf you watched and remember now,
a twisted loop of purple sliding off into water.
                What can I remember?

Dragonflies, everywhere, tipping their tails together,
and the cottonwoods
                sending their snow down the wind...

and what I couldn't see,
what I imagined to be the first time two bodies

lay down naked in the sun beneath an invisible eye,
the woman's body, as it should,
                dividing and re-dividing,

and finally, the fish,
when I knelt down to bathe, swimming out of the rocks
to feed on what we spilled.

Infecundity

To say what's normal
is to say that in snow the cellar doors unfold
                              like white, unfeathering wings,
and that down there in jars are the earth's blooms,
the wound green borne to fruit,
                              what I'll always desire,
suspended, as deathless in the sealed dark
as what floated like dreams in the jars of my classroom
days,
                              globular, transparent,
the veined embryos of what I could hardly name,
but could hold in my hands,
                              re-wombed and expectant
in their glass sacs,
what had thickened the pig's teat. It was so easy then.

I could bear them again and again
as I stood young and almost fertile in the jar's dizzy air,
                              the bud of something whole
delivered to my tabletop
                              to be pinned and probed.
Snakes, half-frogs, pigs
scooped out of time
                              to hang pale and distended
forever
until I pulled them back in to slit their bellies,
all those poisoned futures
                              unpiecing one by one
into my own.

At the Ruins of the Aztec Goddess Ix-Chel
for G.T.

As if there were purpose,

a gauze of rain floats, I know, like child's breath
through the dark fingers of some far pine,

or the flood-riven rocks, chasms of no light,
the piled alters of earth

we have laid our bodies to for so long.
Hope is like this, I think, and prayer.

All night I think of you, the weight of your child
here and now, and his precarious living,

your wants, that shame me,
as simple as decay—

his sickness like soon-fallen leafs of fever
beneath the shaken winter of your hands.

What I want is the lifting of absence,
the blind root flowering through the body

as it does the earth and those tiny pockets of breath
the vanished have given it,

the sealed fruits of my summer
made open and living in the easy air.

Coming here, I see we are no different
from those women past,

pilgrims stroking the blue world,
the hopeful and the hopeless paddling oceans,

the stretched skins of their boats
light over the buoyant water,

the beached and virginal sands of this island,
made holy by mud and shell,

like light, too, and breath,
as woman after woman on the night's shore

lie down the same, naked and alone
in the spreading silver, the warm salt.

Day of Atonement

Whenever I crouch over you, my body
jailed by the slatted light, you take the soles of my feet
in hand and rub the ground-thickened flesh, the pale star,
scar of the nail that hurts me still.

Today is the day sin turns to bread,
the day the Jews of our neighborhood, who shun me,
goyim, toss the stale dredgings of their lives to the lake,
to the fowl, to the geese that hunch their hinged shoulders
against an air that lets nothing rise with ease.

And all day they've passed by our window, stony
and black, passed the bed where we saucer our bodies
in the same broken-down hollows your aunts—old maid
Jews, (is there a word for this?) —shared all their nights,

where we want to believe their bodies had something more
than the final stitching of the throat, something more
than even us, who could bear for them again and again,
but have thrust ourselves into their house and stripped
                from the world, even the door jamb, the
caulking they once bandaged to healing.

Sunset, the lake smoothed to shell,
the Jews stand in tennis shoes among the battered cattail,
reading their prayers to the gill-slitted fish
that leap and fan for what we breathe, the water I have
walked in
                bone-gasping, and the shored rocks
netted to moss where soon birds will bank themselves
and leave a tattered snowfield. Come, let me crawl
beneath you, and let what loves you
                reap our sins.

Garage

There was light, brittle,
thin husks of sun
strewn over the dark pitch
of the asphalt and the smooth metals of cars.

We had been to the river, its bent grasses:
the slow dive of our bodies,
the endless moon pitch
cell by cell toward water
and the small spears
of the river fish breaking through.

But we loved others,
or others loved us, or did not.
And so we did not touch.
We walked home together
and did not touch
until finally in the flat light
we stood at the oiled edge
of that borrowed garage.

There was no window.
We did not switch on
the webbed halo
of that one bulb, but together,
hand over hand, jerked down the door,
its wheels stuttering
over the bare rails of the day,
the small stones of our bodies
paling among the dark cements, the hard,
thread-worn stacks of tires, the hooked ladders.

You knelt before me.
I felt the small of my back open,
petals of flesh,
the tiny moons of the body
beneath the willed hand, yoked.
You touched me there.

And then the rib's slender graft
uncaged the heart's sprawl
and spore mulch salt—tart garden of my body—
rivered my blue veins.

The small heats of your moon body
pass over me.

Why I Do Not Go

This love then, this body, this torn off
in living but death, what you can not
leave. Like the cicada, an unknown
stirring, palpable, splits the skin
not wholly, but part, behind the dark
cage of the heart open now to air
to any thing that might strike it. I
remember crawling out of the dark-
ness, my body still warm, still slick in

its shining, but crushed, given over.
There were strange sounds, my mother's voice, rains
bitter, heart drenched in a skin of rain,
and me entangled still. A child's
word, *puddle*, but for us now, you said,
drenched ground, flooded abyss. I remember
the small pocket curves of your elbows,
of your knees when I leaned over you,
rained down over your whole body. And

then the rise, love's curve, and the wings bent
once, pouring me into the blue rags
of sky. Do you see how every piece
of me then, split, is intact, ghost
of my old body, the curved empty
abdomen, and, like clear glass, the eyes
broken? What do we have after? There
is love and it bursts out of the ground
only once and this is what you die for.

III

Snow drifts in the shadow
places of the bone.
I go down to the river.
Winter stalks me.
Its fierce staffs hone the air,
skeletal, broken.
Why did I think this thaw
should bring only spring,
those delicate pinpoints
of purple mustard,
evening star
wavering at the world's feet
redemptive, sure?
Beneath the bare cottonwood,
beneath the wild plum,
there is a tiny spray of bone—
jaw and the fine rings of spine,
claw of the wintering bird
the owl in darkness
stills into quiet wing
and dark mouth.
I hold in my hand
this pellet of owl,
mouse of field,
blue shell
of crawdad.
Can you hear the river's tongue?
The husks of winter
are breaking like delicate ships
the wind steers,
and already
beneath shining seed
pale blossoms
small as the heart
(and this mine)
tremble.

It Is Spring, Yes

Perhaps because all winter
in the night clock's dim blue,
that tide pool where moonless our dreamed selves
floated on the edge of air,

and night after night, I felt your body move
with lessening hope over mine,
I cannot yet think how it is spring,
but take too hard

this shrill clash of mallard,
the first soft air, that I at last bared the pale winter
of my body to,
gone harsh with this sounding.

The ducks careen too low through the new drifts
of oak leaf, the males, bottle-green and beautiful,
tip hard against the female's wing fan
until one by one they skid into the blue

wishless coin of water to mount
half drowned and drowning.
It is spring, yes, but I forget still
how in just one night,

as the last scythes of snow
waned beneath the blue spruce and red wings
first flared through the pale webs of cattails,
we were twice blessed, your two children

stirring even now loved beneath my heart.
Or how very soon it will be that I will lie down
as in childhood, as in the girl
who once waited through whole summers

to lie down beneath the last golds
bursting from the slow-sapping trees,
and watched then in loneliness the leaving flocks,
those slow arrows of farewell.

Incubations

I would take you sleeping from your glass box,
the wrinkled prunes of your knees drawn still to your chest
where once the delicate sacs of your lungs
closed and flowered and closed
with the endless sea-fill of my near heart,
and where now a wing, so small it's not even a bird's,
in a clasp of ribs, shivers, beneath my finger, with new air.

They have taught me how to do this, how to lower this door
and slide carefully toward me the white tray you lay on,
to take from the shelf the two cloths I will wrap you in,
my left hand cradling the frail shell of your head
and the limp neck where the windpipe, like a thistle,
bends, and my right hand fills with the rest of you,
the fleshless legs, the wrinkles of your unmounded sex, the
flat belly, the navel's stump,
your skin so thin the whole of your body flushes
like some desert clay the sun lights.

And I hold you as if unborn,
you who will not yet open your eyes,
who will not yet look at me,
and when they let me, I take the thin cords that hook you
to the softly beeping machine that says
yes, you are breathing, you are here,
and I pass them safely over us, and then I
hold you to my breast, and, more sure than me, it fills
with the blue milk I have waited my whole life for,
and sometimes, with a touch, you take it.

Early Labors

If I think of it now, I think of spring's
last frost, how the stealing white binds the dark
unsingled grasses and the pale violet,
            and of the newborn that spring,
when mine was still quickening,
thrown warm and steaming over a back fence
to stiffen all night beneath scarce stars.
            And of the woman, not the girl-child
bleeding quietly in her room, only herself again,
but of the woman next door, alone, readying herself
for sleep like she always does, the house darkening itself
around her,
            and herself emptying into dream,
while, familiar as wind, the earth's breath stills, and a
child dies
            beneath her window.

Loss was so certain, and I would stand there
at my window in the bone-crepe of the moon
or the streetlight's unpiecing dark, my body
            that would forgive us nothing flexing you
down and down. Yes, there was your heart,
and the small parts of you, clear and light-filled,
your hand all glass and sea animal,
            and you, too soon at the world's edge.
I would stand there at my window, night after night,
counting, *now this moment, and yes, this one too gone*
and you still safe inside me, until finally,
            like some clanging dawn,
our newspaper woman would pass us by once more,
                        her stolen cart.

But now it is good and I can go into you
and it is night. And I lean way down over the rails
of your crib to hear the tiny dew of your breath,
and the shining fish of your eye
glimmers in the wake of air I leave,
and I think how I was the whole world once
and the sky without stars, your father sleeping
        quietly beside me whole nights, whole months
not knowing how lightly you stepped down.

Blizzard

Already the hunters of elk,
of spar and rut, sag beneath this first
weight of snow. They are lost.

All day I opened the blinds to see it come,
the first storm of our prairied winter
brooding over the wintered peaks
like a thumb bruise.

Snow clusters in the wallows
of the elk, in the wintering ground.
Night enters the white paper
of the girdled birch,
and the fine combs of aspen
bend over double, threshers
of August velvet, honers
of the bone's great rack.

And now the first blow
and the gold lanterns of the cottonwood
flicker over the brown yard.
Here is the breath of my hand
on the glass and the ice climbing.
In this borrowed room, there is a lonely
woman's bed where sometimes I lay with you,
your arms around me sometimes.
Those two sisters, I cannot forget them,
their quiet undressing
fills the room, night after night,
the hushed folding of their dresses,
and sometimes the hall's light, or the moon
pushed back,
entering to touch them.

The magpie
in black and white tips from the brink of trees
and the hunter sights down the rib.
He would have the cape of this animal.

They share your father's blood
and yours and here, now, in the warm sleeping dark,
they are the moth-stir at the fluted bones
of our two early daughters, their wrists
smaller than your thumb.

  This is winter's bugle
and I watch winter hurling itself
beneath the streetlamps, arced and sulfurous,
its thick pelt brushed over the angled roofs
of our feeders, the frail stems
of the cherry and the pear bending to earth,
and I go without reason to stand in our yard
full-faced against the wind
without coat or glove, those thick wheels
of snow raking all over me.

  The wintered hunters search
  for the snow's unbalance, the heart track.
  Aged, it is the hoar crystal,
  the dust's fine pock,
  the fresh dark breath
  of the morning soil upturned.

And here, where the black peaks
of houses in summer shadow the lighted air,
and unleash the second stars,
I watch you through the window,
through the dishes' steam.

Sleeping with Our Daughters

*–In REM sleep, the large voluntary muscles are paralyzed
to prevent dreamers from acting out their dreams.*

Our daughters ride our shoulders like angels.
They are dreaming the blue smell

of the breast, its warm milk pores,
the womb and its salts.

We are sleeping. A half-life of dreams
and our hearts open surely for their dark air.

Our muscles beneath their red waters
flex and still.

And now the primitive stem
of the brain, its old haunts—ape and ground squirrel,

the stepping fish—fires its aimless fires.
We give them tongue:

Mother. Father. The *Cave* and its boarded windows,
Bird and *Cone* stir through the stems of our fingers.

We are wound about the spindles of the tree.
We hang above the dark pockets of the Garden,

God's breath, cold and heavy, sliding past where we root,
wrathless past blossoms, those bee-nailed corals.

And now the same dream begins:
the stairs, they are sharp and disinterested.

They beckon down. There is no railing.
And here is the false weight of our children.

They lie quietly in our hands, asleep
in their soft flannels, the shrouds

we have wrapped for them.
Here is gravity's betrayal, its dizzy pitch

and we are stepping down.
They have grafted your arms to a dwarf

and nailed you to a trellis. You are the netted sun,
evergreen, orange wind, the sea's spindrift

that nets the white root and the navel.
Our daughters are falling from our hands

and our muscles freeze us to our beds.
We will not move.

Is this what I want, over and over again?
How many times, in the quiet dark

of your bed, have you killed them,
your body, reflexive, kicking you back?

Your seed trembles in the core's canal.
Oh, here is your red flesh and your white heart.

Roto-Rooter Man

I stand with him above my winter basement,
above the stairs, bare planks
like the stuttered troughs of river
I'll ferry him dog-worried down.
To think day after day that this
is what he wants—to go under,
to stand at the black poplar inked in the river's slide,
one more bitter coin cool beneath his tongue.
I am the woman beside him, smiling.
Her hands worry her white apron.
They are warm and wet
with the bathing of her children.
She steams and rubs their pink skins,
the fair cocoons where strangers twitch.
The cellar air rises cool, eclipsed.
I see the stars in endless night reeling,
the jittering bats, shrill, faceless,
oceans frozen.
I am leading him down to the bare joists,
the swept cement, the underwear
we've strewn naked in flower wilt, the sun
in its green box that fires this house.
We have frayed. Hair, our skin
cellular, pungent slough down
our sinks and tubs. And now the drain coughs
and a tiny pocket of spring
mulches the floor at our feet.
This is what he knows—
the very center, the heart
in its cellar darkness,
the earthnut, the taproot, the blind steel
of the tubar that works our frail metals.

Above us, the world is only pieces:
roofs and the rungs of steadied ladders,
the tar's heat, the lean-to and the pitch,
the nailed shingles, the shadow's noon root.
The shoes of my children thump the floorboards.
Their voices splinter. He is uncoiling his cables
to shunt our pipes clear
and I wait for him.

The Weasel Sandman

Neither doubt its truth nor its dream of truth.
                    –Johann Gottfried Herder

In a square of light, the silver ash
is singing.
And the crawdad moon, the blue
underbelly of its claws
back-scuttles the bucket sky.

My daughters' faces glow
in the balloon light. They color air.
They cannot see me.
They press their faces
against the thin black screen of their window
I have shaken the lock of again and again.

This is the snow of corn,
their third summer,
and my daughters want me to scare them.
They want the three bears
to tumble down the hollow
tree again and again, the alligator
to once more open
its long ticking mouth.

I want to tell them something
sweet, something about flowers,
their long tunnels, the light knots
of their pollen, how sometimes
moths like hummingbirds
will whirl through their rafters,
and ours.

But they want the bite.
They want it dark.
They want the weasel sandman,
the sun like a plate tipping
past the one good hill
and its two cottonwoods
that keep us from seeing round.

And now the first star
blinks in. Night
showers us with its gold coins.
The sandman is prowling the wet
corners of our neighborhood.
The reed voices of children
are reeling him in.
His sand is dangerous and beautiful.
This is what they dream.

Dark, I hear my daughters say,
it real dark outside.
You see, *the very blood talks*.
And the giant's shoes,
that thunder
shuffling over the small
white strings of our hearts,
fall one by one.

Queen Bee

When that bee stung you, when that
forager thrust into your thumb its mock ovipositor,

your thumb admits all the other pink
and dark thumbs blossoming on that bus,

that worker ferrying through sudden
blue windows of air its thousand flowers,

and you in your winter sleep,

the pain you said was like never before.
what you said to me was

You never felt pain like this before, me
with that surgeon's gash etched above my pubic bone,

my daughters pulled one by one
out of the slit sac of my belly.

Well, I'll tell you, I felt that.

I felt that hard snatch into light and air,
the surgeon's tug stitching me back. And that night,

morphine ticking down my veins,
I stepped down the flower's tongue.

I was no queen.
I was her sterile daughter,

the night nurse tip-toeing into my room to check
my heat and my bleeding, and me asking her,

Am I mother?

You did not even breathe.
The mapped yawn of the world floated beneath me,

the sun's weight measurable, its light danceable.
I stood at the door of the hive.

I felt the kiss of my sisters,
the taste of my mother.

And then I saw my wrapped daughters
in their glass cells.

Husband, Father, Brother, Son,
you are stepping huge-eyed out of the purpling wax,

the comb pendulous, brooding. You would have the mother.
Her light feet spiral over the clean cells

she has built. She will have you once.
Her eggs are white and glistening.

Mira's Dream

You picked that special flower and it lit up and I thought
it was a lightening bug and then it flew into my eye.

The world is lines and circles.
My fingertips are whorls of deadwood.
See the river? It is an 'S', black snake,
and it slides beneath the ice, circles like white scales.
I take his children into the woods.
The trees cage the sky
with their great empty branches.
There is no mother to be perfect.
She can only be the moon, that light
rolling down the thatched steeples of the roof,
the boy peering over his shoulder again
and again, bread crumbling from his hands
like small moons thieves of birds will lift singing.
My children quiet. We stand on a path
of snow, "old" I tell them, and it bears
heavy grain like circles.
I hear the hard clap of wood on wood,
chop of the wood cutter
that eased the boy and his sister into dark.
Far out from the trees, the red lights of cars
through the dusk like faint fires float.
Is this what I am? What wounds the heart,
then vanishes? My children speak of heaven.
It is a circle blue that spins above their fenced yard
where the neighbor's dead dog flies on freckled wings.
They do not want it for me.
But there is a hunger. It burns in the belly.
Sometimes I think he can not love me,
his children bending over him,
shaking out from their pockets
shining gold coins.

River Swim

You will not remember this—
the river, its blue stalks of heron,

or how I was everything to you once
at the river's edge, our walking here

on egg smooth stones like the carried heart
of the mountain, unpieced.

Blue sky fills the hollowed earth
and I take you into water.

I have nothing to do with your growing now—
not the white stellar snow of your bones

nor your heart, light-flashed,
Sacred Lily of a thousand years, small seed

unfurling into white root and stem,
false leaf and true.

What has your mother sold
to have you? Where is the dark river

ice of gypsy, what the cells thrust for,
water of me in which you once floated?

Always in dreams, I forget you.
I stand here in the river now, holding you,

your body cool and sky-tinged,
half-weight, half-light.

I am sending you out.
I am teaching you to go under,

to hold under your breath,
to blow out slowly what the heart

all your life has taken in.
Unimaginable this state,

this going under and dreamless,
and still the going on—around you always

the river in spring flood and the hard
winter red branches at root in pained waking.

The green of the world falls over you.
I feel the cage of your body tremble.

I don't want to die
I don't want to die
you whisper in my ear,

then kick off, your slight body
ploughing through the river green.

Dark Birds

What I come back to always
is this: the still dark
house of your breathing
I cannot enter.
            Dark birds   moon ruined.
How can I say anything
of beauty to you?
            Not *staccato rain*
nor *september grasshopper*
nor how the green earth
the green leaf
by faint light
undrowns.

All night I have dreamed
of the blue
butterfly of tornado,
that dark spiral
you know nothing of
but weep over night after night
into my helpless arms.
            River we have been,
your father and I,
green lucidity that has bathed you
since first light.
            It is only wind,

I want to say, *some dark tear*
my hand held to the broken sky
can block with five fingers.
I do not tell you
how it can suck hide

from a cow,
drive splintered wood
through rock,
suck the breath clean out of you,
your heart imploded.
     It's nothing   I say.

     How many nights
have I sat on your bed
Medusa beneath the moon,
and you leaning against me?
     Is everything about Icthus now
that world beneath the world?
Already, within the bleached
sticks of my ribs,
air hushes, gathers.
How can I tell you—
     your father a stone
and I will unmoon the sky?

I stand at your doorway now
and do not breathe
to hear you breathe.
This is a strange green
blooming and I feel
the world turn and turn.
     You are rolling in the dark
and I am listening
to hear the words some god
has given you,
fierce god of your father,
forgotten god of your mother,
your mouth, my rosebud,
womb of my womb
kissing the dark.